Wellington

*An illustrated life of Arthur Wellesley,
first Duke of Wellington*

1769-1852

Amoret and Christopher Scott

Shire Publications Ltd.

2

Contents

Rapid ascent	5
The Peninsular campaigns	9
Waterloo	19
Parliamentary career	27
The final years	37
The principal events of Wellington's life	46
Bibliography	47
Index	48

ACKNOWLEDGEMENTS

The authors and publishers wish to thank the following for permission to reproduce the illustrations on the pages indicated: National Portrait Gallery, 2; Wellington Museum, 13, 17, 28 (lower), 33 (right); Victoria and Albert Museum, 15 (left and right), 16 (left and right), 26; the Duke of Wellington, 21; Peter Grugeon, 28 (top), 43 (top); Lady Longford, 33 (lower left); A. C. Cooper Ltd., 40; Department of the Environment, 43 (bottom); Miss Barbara Murray and C. R. Leslie Esq., 45 (photograph arranged by Lady Longford). The illustration on page 10 is from Bradford's 'Views of the War in the Peninsula'; that on page 34 was originally published in 1829 by T. McLean; that on page 35, engraving published 1834 by T. McLean (photograph arranged by the Wellington Museum).

The cover design by Robin Ollington shows 'A Wellington Boot', a caricature of Wellington as Commander-in-Chief of the Army, 1827.

Copyright © 1973 by Amoret and Christopher Scott. First published October 1973, reprinted 1984. ISBN 0 85263 239 8.

No part of this publication may be reproduced or transmitted in any form or by any means, electronic or mechanical, including photocopy, recording, or any information storage and retrieval system, without permission in writing from the publishers, Shire Publications Ltd, Cromwell House, Church Street, Princes Risborough, Aylesbury, Bucks, HP17 9AJ, UK.

Printed by C. I. Thomas & Sons (Haverfordwest) Ltd., Merlins Bridge, Haverfordwest.

Opposite: Major-General the Hon. Sir Arthur Wellesley, 1804.

Rapid ascent

BACKGROUND AND EARLY YEARS 1769—1796
By an accident of history, the two leading actors in the struggle for Europe which came about forty years later were both born in the same year, 1769: Napoleon Bonaparte in Corsica and Arthur Wesley (whose name was changed to Wellesley twenty-nine years later) in Dublin.

Arthur was one of seven children of the Earl of Mornington. His parents regarded all the others as brighter and more likely to succeed: the effect, or perhaps the cause, was that he was 'dreamy, idle and shy' (his own words in later life) as a boy, suffering from poor health and living a lonely and withdrawn existence at school. Almost the only gift he inherited from his father was a love of music, which led to considerable skill on the violin. It was to be one of the most significant acts of his life when at the age of twenty-four, as a young lieutenant-colonel at the crossroads of a career, he burned that violin, symbolically destroying the refuge which might prevent him from becoming exposed to the fires which would temper his character. In the same act, he destroyed his youth.

There was little enough pleasure in it. When he was twelve his father died. In the same year he went to Eton but at the age of fifteen he was taken away, having made a poor showing at both studies and games, to make room for his two younger and more brilliant brothers. His mother, during a period of some financial difficulties, took him to Brussels (where the living was cheaper) for a year and then, almost as a last resort, decided that the awkward boy was only fit for the Army. In preparation, he was sent to a French military and riding school at Angers for a year in 1786.

Opposite: A silhouette of Arthur Wesley, c.1780, shortly before he was sent to Eton. One of seven children, Arthur was 'dreamy, idle and shy'.

Wellington

At once a new purpose seemed to enter his life. He returned, speaking good French and with an excellent seat on a horse, and was gazetted ensign in the 73rd Highland Regiment in 1787. With family influence and financial help (somewhat more difficult to extract) he bought his way quickly up the ranks of the army in the established way of the time. The same influence took him as aide-de-camp to the Lord Lieutenant of Ireland, and to an election as MP in the family seat of Trim in the Irish Parliament. In 1793 he purchased the lieutenant-colonelcy of the 33rd Foot (now the Duke of Wellington's Regiment) and burnt his violin. In the following year his regiment was sent to Belgium, and the future field-marshal saw his first action against the French.

INDIA 1796–1805

Returning to Dublin in 1796 he followed his regiment to India, now a full colonel. For nine years he had suffered the intrigues and the repressive atmosphere of court life as lived in Dublin, and a symbolic wind to freshen his outlook was overdue. The long voyage to India seems to have achieved a rapid hardening of both his physique and his character, and the new horizons opening before him were wide and exciting. At all events he was a person to be reckoned with almost as soon as he arrived, and when his eldest brother Lord Mornington was appointed Governor-General of India his position was reinforced, as was his name (the new Viceroy reverted to an older spelling of the family name, becoming the Marquess of Wellesley, and Arthur was obliged to follow suit).

Impatient to put his military studies to the test, Wellesley suffered considerable frustrations in his early years in India, but in 1799 he was given command of the expedition against Tippoo Sultan, ruler of Mysore and supported by the French. After some initial reverses Wellesley laid siege to Seringapatam and his force captured in in fine style. (Also captured was Tippoo's musical tiger, which is now on display at the Victoria and Albert Museum.) In 1805 began the Second Mahratta War, a confrontation between Wellesley's troops and a French-supported and French-trained coalition of Indian rulers. The war came to a head at the battle of Assaye in September 1803. Seven thousand British and native troops defeated an enemy of about forty thousand, almost entirely through the

Assaye

tactical judgement and nerve of Wellesley. 'The General was in the thick of the action the whole time ... I never saw a man so cool and collected as he was ...' wrote one of his officers after the battle. To the end of his life he regarded the victory at Assaye as his finest military achievement. But even then he was grieving at the slaughter involved and throughout his career his officers saw him, after almost every bloody battle, overcome at the tragic waste of brave lives.

In 1805 Sir Arthur Wellesley (he had been made a Knight of the Bath for the victory at Assaye) left India for ever. In the nine years of his service he had risen in rank to major-general, and had accumulated experience which was to prove invaluable in the European conflict that was developing in these early years of the new century: experience of sieges, rapid movement and guerrilla warfare; of civilian administration; of the politics and in-fighting of command; and of the importance of supplies and physical toughness. On the voyage home, significantly he spent a month on St Helena where Napoleon was to die in exile as a direct result of Wellesley's military brilliance.

INTERLUDE AND MARRIAGE 1805–1808

In the interval before starting on his first fateful journey to the Peninsula, Wellesley was elected to Parliament again – this time in England, for Rye – did a few odd military jobs and in 1806 married Katherine Pakenham with whom he had had a vague understanding ever since his service in Ireland. He had proposed once before, in those impecunious and unspectacular days of his comparative youth, and had been refused. He was now a rising star, major-general, K.B., and a prize worth winning. Sadly, however, the marriage was a failure almost from the beginning; she was unable to match the speed of his ascent and their temperaments were anything but well-matched. It was almost the only serious error of judgement in his life; Kitty's anxious, intellectually limited character grated on him continually, and their moments of happiness were few and short.

His energies and interests were soon devoted to a new job – Chief Secretary of Ireland, a post which threw him into the deep end of politics. But he was still a soldier, and the call of action on the continent was a good deal stronger than a lucrative position in Dublin or a comparatively new marriage.

Wellington

His next chance came with the formation in 1807 of an expedition to seize the neutral Danish fleet in Copenhagen, which Napoleon seemed likely to capture for use against England. Wellesley commanded a brigade and once again distinguished himself. (It was during this campaign that a mare belonging to Lord Grosvenor was found to be in foal and was sent back to England; the chestnut foal was named Copenhagen, and was bought later by Wellesley, in 1810. Copenhagen remained his favourite horse, dying in 1836 in honourable retirement at Stratfield Saye where he is buried under a moving epitaph.)

Home again after a successfully concluded campaign, Wellesley returned to the Irish scene in his former position as Chief Secretary. In 1808, at the age of forty, he was promoted to lieutenant-general. Then, just as he was about to lead an ill-advised expedition to South America to help an uprising against France's ally, Spain, in the Spanish colonies, Napoleon made the fatal mistake of ousting the popular King Ferdinand VII of Spain and replacing him with his own brother, Joseph Bonaparte. Spain, uneasy ally of Napoleon that she was, rose in rebellion. England, seeing her chance, diverted the expedition from South America to Corunna in north-western Spain. The future Duke of Wellington, instead of disappearing to an almost certain fiasco, went to meet his destiny – characteristically starting to learn Spanish on the voyage.

The Peninsular campaigns

BATTLE OF VIMEIRO
Wellesley's 9,000 troops, plus a further 5,000 waiting for him in Spain, were good material, though weak in cavalry numbers. Just before he set out, the government at home realised that the problem of the French in Spain and Portugal was a good deal bigger than they had initially thought, and announced that a further 15,000 troops were to be sent – and that Wellesley would have to step down for a more senior commander. Swallowing his disappointment and disquiet – for his cool assessment told him that he could conduct a better campaign than the elderly seniors about to be placed over him – he landed some way north of Lisbon (Portugal was entirely occupied by the French except for a few pockets of resistance) on 1st August 1808, and prepared to march on the capital.

After some skirmishes and one small battle at Roliça, Wellesley reached the coastal village of Vimeiro where some of the reinforcing troops, including his replacement as commander, Sir Henry Burrard, disembarked. Almost at once a large French force marched out of its enormously strong position (which was to assume much greater importance two years later) at Torres Vedras, the mountains north of Lisbon, to take the British force by surprise. The battle of Vimeiro was fought on 21st August 1808. The British infantry repeatedly routed their French counterparts by attacking from concealed positions behind the crest of a hill; the cavalry was more spectacular but far less effective. The victory won by Wellesley was thrown away by the caution of Sir Henry Burrard who refused to follow up the rout of the French. Wellesley, disgusted, announced to his staff that they might as well go and shoot partridges: which they did.

It was Wellesley's first major encounter with seasoned French troops, undisputed masters of the battlefields of Europe, and his success, wasted though it was, gave him enormous

The lines of Torres Vedras, Wellington's brilliantly conceived defensive system, behind which he withdrew in the winter of 1810–1811.

confidence in both himself and his men. The direct result of Vimeiro was an armistice and the agreed evacuation of the whole of Portugal by the French, but under terms which disgusted Britain by their leniency. Wellesley, though now a subordinate commander, had signed this Convention of Cintra, and he received many of the brickbats. It was his first (but by no means his last) taste of the fickleness and fury of the public at home. The generals whose caution had caused the situation he castigated in private, but his principles would not allow him to do so in public. He refused to defend his conduct of the campaign in any way, a characteristic which became more marked in his political career later.

In October 1808 he was back in England and, still being Chief Secretary, Ireland. His thoughts were in the Peninsula, however, for major events were happening in Spain during his absence. Napoleon had taken a vice-like grip of the country. Sir John Moore, one of England's few really able commanders, had been killed at Corunna during a Dunkirk-like evacuation after a long retreat and once again Portugal was full of French soldiers.

Return to Portugal

FULL AUTHORITY AND TALAVERA

In March 1809 the government turned to Wellesley to command an expeditionary force with the object of rescuing Portugal for a second time. This time he was given the full authority for which he had longed and now he symbolically burned his boats, as he had done his violin years before, resigning his seat in Parliament and his lucrative office as Chief Secretary of Ireland, to which he had given sporadic attention between campaigns. He sailed for Portugal on 14th April, in command at last, hardly imagining that he was not to set foot in Britain again for five years.

Immediately on his arrival in Portugal, he set out to capture Oporto from the French under Marshal Soult. By surprise tactics and with almost no loss of life he not only took Oporto in the action known as the Passage of the Douro, but proceeded to chase the whole French army out of Portugal; it took just four weeks from his first arrival. At the Spanish border he stopped in accordance with his strict orders. This allowed Soult to escape to fight again, and the spectre of Cintra was raised again in England. By this time Wellesley had grown a thicker skin.

In July, armed with fresh orders and a replenished treasury (Wellesley knew the importance of a population friendly to him and his army paid for what they took, unlike Napoleon's troops) he crossed into Spain on the road leading to Madrid. A hundred miles on he joined forces with a Spanish army under General Cuesta, in pursuit of a French army commanded by Marshal Victor. Cuesta's troops were undisciplined and, for much of the time, an active hindrance to Wellesley. With careful diplomacy with his ally and his remarkable eye for ground he succeeded on 28th July 1809 in facing the French – 40,000 to his own combined force of 20,000 – on ground of his choosing at the town of Talavera, about 70 miles west of Madrid. It was a desperate and bloody battle, filled with crises, which lasted two days and (unusually in those times of daylight battles) most of one night; it cost 7,000 French lives and 5,000 British and Spanish ones. At the end of it the French had retired towards Madrid and Wellesley was left not only victorious but ennobled. A grateful nation created him Viscount Wellington of Talavera on 4th September.

He knew, as England did not, how transitory such a victory

was. 'Don't halloo until you are out of the wood' he wrote in response to a particularly fulsomely inscribed portrait. And in fact, by the time news of his viscountcy reached him, Wellington was retreating. Within a few weeks he was back in Portugal with the memory of Talavera dim, a sour government at home and a furious ally in Spain. He had no choice but a retreat: every French army in Spain was making for him and his long lines of communication were horribly vulnerable. But the fickle public raised the old cry again, and accusations of being unable to finish the job were levelled at him. Throughout his military career he distrusted and, as far as he could, ignored the politicians who were his masters. Given enough supplies and men, he had developed a cold and rational confidence in his ability to defeat the enemy.

WITHDRAWAL TO TORRES VEDRAS

Back in Lisbon he watched while the Spanish army was completely routed in November; by February 1810 the only resistance to King Joseph Bonaparte came from guerrillas, who played a very significant part in the pinning down of the huge French force (350,000 men) scattered through Spain under the command of two formidable marshals of France – Massena and Ney. During the summer of 1810 Massena advanced into Portugal. Wellington withdrew before him, leaving a 'scorched earth' countryside that the French found extremely trying. At the end of September he stopped, hidden behind a long steep ridge at Bussaco, about 50 miles south of Oporto.

The battle which followed was another desperate contest which could easily have been won by the French. Wellington's masterly use of ground and the steadiness and gallantry of the Portuguese, as well as the British, finally threw back Massena's troops with heavy losses. But this victory was merely a bonus in his planned withdrawal into the mountainous natural fortress country of Portugal, where he could build up strength to go on the offensive when the time was ripe. Immediately he continued his retreat, followed by the French, down the road towards Lisbon. But while Massena was convinced that Wellington would be driven headlong into the sea, he was in fact making for the brilliantly conceived system of defences and fortifications he had constructed during the period of apparent inactivity.

These were the lines of Torres Vedras, an impregnable series

Wellington at the storming of Ciudad Rodrigo in 1812, a French-held fortress just inside Spain, and long a thorn in his flesh.

of strongpoints in a landscape of soaring sharp crags. The French, knowing nothing about this vast fortress, in spite of their considerable intelligence system, ran headlong into its outposts and then sat for four months wondering what to do, while the starvation created by the scorched-earth policy of Wellington grew into a nightmare. Finally, in the middle of March 1811, Massena abandoned his position; his retreat accelerated northwards, then eastwards, harassed by masterly skirmishes from Wellington, until within a month the French were driven out of Portugal again. The lines of Torres Vedras had cost Napoleon a staggering 25,000 dead, against Wellington's 4,000. In its conception and execution this was possibly Wellington's greatest military achievement, and it had a profound effect on the war as a whole.

ALBUERA AND SALAMANCA

Spain, however, was still firmly under Napoleon's thumb, and just across the border from Portugal were two fortresses:

Wellington

Badajoz in the south and Ciudad Rodrigo in the north. From the latter, in May, came a determined assault over the river frontier at Fuentes de Onoro to relieve the one fortress town in Portugal still in French hands, Almeida. Another gory and frighteningly close battle sent Massena's troops back to Ciudad Rodrigo. At Badajoz, British forces under General Beresford laid siege to the fortress at about the same time. Almost at once the French under Soult marched to relieve it, and a particularly bloody battle was fought at Albuera in which the French lost nearly a third, and the British and Spanish nearly half of their troops. Soult retired and Albuera was recorded as a British victory, Pyrrhic though it was, and Badajoz was still occupied by the French. Wellington sped south to direct another siege of the city but was equally unsuccessful. In August he marched back to Ciudad Rodrigo with a determination to go on to the offensive.

But he had to wait. Months were needed to build up his army, depleted from battles and sickness. Not until January 1812 was he able to lay siege again to Ciudad Rodrigo, and this time it went without a hitch. Wellington was created an earl by the British government, and Duke of Ciudad Rodrigo by the Spanish. Badajoz was less easily captured, but it too fell in April with frightful losses on both sides. The roads to Madrid were open at last.

In June the army of about 46,000 British, Portuguese and Spanish troops set off along the road to Salamanca, which had to be blockaded before giving in. The army of Marmont (Massena's successor) waited not far away and Wellington watched, once again behind a ridge. The armies waited for three solid weeks of manoeuvre and counter-manoeuvre, until on 22nd July the battle of Salamanca was fought. This time, thanks to a fatal mistake by Marmont in extending his line too far, and some magnificent British cavalry charges to take advantage of the lapse, the victory was clear-cut and rapid. 14,000 French troops were casualties, against 5,000 Allied soldiers. Without further ado Wellington marched on the hundred miles to Madrid where he and his army were received as heroes and more honours were heaped on him – a Marquessate, a Spanish estate near Granada.

There followed a period of frustration and set-backs. Trying to catch and defeat the French 'Portuguese army', Wellington

Left: The battle of Salamanca, 22nd July 1812, here depicted on part of the Berlin Service, was a clear-cut victory for Wellington.

Right: Joseph Bonaparte, King of Spain. His appointment as King by his brother Napoleon caused the Spanish to rebel and thereby prompted the British to fight the Peninsular campaigns.

became involved in another siege (always his weakest point because of the lack of good sappers and proper equipment), this time at Burgos, 120 miles north of Madrid. After a month of ineffectual attempts he gave up. Napoleon's retreat from Moscow marked the beginning of a bad time: French armies totalling 100,000 were closing on Wellington and once again he found himself at Salamanca, and then right back to Ciudad Rodrigo with an army not far off being a rabble, ill-disciplined and miserable in the foul weather of November. Luckily, things improved once they were all in winter quarters with food, tobacco and rest. Wellington even got in some hunting, which remained a great pleasure to him throughout his campaigns whenever he had the time and the opportunity.

VITORIA AND THE PYRENEES

At the end of May 1813, refreshed, re-equipped and with new plans known only to himself (he had decided through bitter experience that actions were the only things that really

15

Left: Arthur Wellesley, first Duke of Wellington, K.G., portrayed in 1814 by Sir Thomas Lawrence.
Right: The Peninsular Gold Cross, with nine clasps (only Wellington had all nine).

counted, though the habit of playing his cards close to his chest was less successful in his political career, as will be seen) the army set out again, apparently towards Salamanca. In fact Wellington's main force marched north through country regarded as virtually impassable and then turned east, creating such uncertainty in Joseph Bonaparte's mind that he evacuated Valladolid and blew up Burgos, retreating towards France. At Vitoria, little more than 50 miles from the Pyrenees, he turned to wait for his tormentor. The battle was fought on 21st June and resulted in a sweeping victory for Wellington at a cost of 5,000 casualties. The French lost 8,000 and a vast quantity of

Vitoria

treasure looted from the Spanish royal palaces, including many pictures from the royal collections. When, shortly afterwards, Wellington made to return these priceless pictures to King Ferdinand VII, he was bidden to keep them and they hang to this day in the Wellington Museum at Apsley House and at Stratfield Saye House. Joseph only escaped by the skin of his teeth, leaping out of one side of his carriage as English Hussars leapt in at the other. But he and his army escaped over the Pyrenees mainly because Wellington's army ('the scum of the earth' as he called them) was enjoying the rich fruits of victory too much to follow it up.

Wellington, on the same principle as that of paying for supplies, was harsh and adamant about plunder and pillage. But the troops after Vitoria were beyond any officer to control. England and Europe were nonetheless ecstatic. Wellington was promoted field-marshal, the Portuguese made him a duke, and Beethoven wrote his atmospheric 'Wellington's Victory'.

In France, a furious Napoleon sacked his brother Joseph and handed the armies back to the redoubtable Soult – who in a fortnight was crossing the mountains again to relieve San Sebastian and Pamplona, the only French pockets left in the Peninsula. For a month from the end of July 1813 minor battles and skirmishes collectively known as the Battles of the Pyrenees were fought. The consequence was inevitable: on 31st August San Sebastian was taken with frightful slaughter. (Pamplona held out for a further two months.)

The battle of Vitoria, 21st June 1813, depicting the capture of the baton of Marshal Jourdain.

Wellington

An exhausted army and an attack of lumbago kept Wellington in Spain until early October, but then he crossed the Pyrenees and entered France at last. Soult expected to stop him at a prepared mountain position above the river Nivelle, but Wellington was not to be stopped until winter, when the cold and the incessant rain did what the French could not do and he settled down in front of Bayonne.

NAPOLEON ABDICATES

In mid-February he was off again, fighting and winning a series of actions against Soult and eventually taking Toulouse (with heavy losses) on 10th April 1814. But on the same day there arrived the news that brought the war to a sudden end: Napoleon had abdicated. In the rejoicing all over Europe which followed, Wellington was made a duke and accepted the position of ambassador in Paris, while Napoleon was exiled to Elba. Wellington's army, which had performed such miracles under his leadership, was disbanded and on 23rd June 1814 the hero returned to England to receive the plaudits and the adulation (which he hated) of the whole country. He was forty-five. At the beginning of August he left to take up his ambassadorial duties in Paris, spending some time on the way there in looking at and thinking about sites for hypothetical battles in Holland and Belgium, one of which was a village called Waterloo.

Wellington moved into a house in Paris (it is still the British Embassy to this day) which he bought from Napoleon's sister, Princess Pauline Borghese. His tasks as ambassador were not particularly onerous. He enjoyed himself a good deal, hunting and keeping the salons of Paris agog with stories (mostly untrue) of liaisons with some of the society ladies who had flocked there. Kitty, his duchess, found the going very hard when she came out to join him. Through the autumn of 1814 Paris became increasingly restive with revived Napoleonic undercurrents, to the extent that there began to be serious fears for Wellington's safety. In January 1815 he was diplomatically, and 'temporarily', sent to Vienna to represent Britain at the congress which was intended to produce a lasting peace in Europe. On 7th March the news reached Vienna that Napoleon had escaped from Elba nine days earlier and the monarchs and statesmen of Europe turned almost as one man to Wellington to save the situation again.

Waterloo

NAPOLEON IN PARIS
France, disgusted and bored by the inefficient decadence of Louis XVIII, had welcomed Bonaparte back with joy. Within three weeks of landing in France, Napoleon was in Paris again as Emperor. At the Congress of Vienna Wellington was appointed Commander-in-Chief of the British, Dutch and Belgian forces, and left at the end of March for Brussels. The forces at his disposal were not impressive: his own Peninsula veterans were largely disbanded (less than 7,000 of the 30,000 British troops now under his command had seen action) and the only other soldiers he trusted were Marshal Blücher's Prussians. Waiting for Napoleon to leave Paris, Wellington spent April and May organising this mixed bag from his headquarters in Brussels. Blücher's headquarters were fifty miles away and the junction of the two armies was a weak point astride the Charleroi-Brussels road; Napoleon knew this, and by the night of 13th June the French armies were camped on the Belgian borders.

QUATRE BRAS 16th JUNE 1815
With 122,000 men against the combined British, Dutch and Prussian force of nearly twice this, Napoleon knew that he had to divide to conquer. The weak point he had noticed between the two main blocks of Allied troops was the crossroads at Quatre Bras. Before dawn on 15th June he had moved into Belgium, and the Prussians out of Charleroi. For once, Wellington had misinterpreted the tactical situation, and was still expecting an attack round his right flank; Napoleon's attack in the middle he regarded as a feint, and his first disposition of troops did little or nothing to help the Prussians. Not until about midnight was the real threat recognised.
Wellington, still in Brussels, issued his orders and then went

Wellington

to the ball which the Duchess of Richmond (one of the large colony of visiting notables) was giving that night. This was not sheer bravado as has often been thought – bravado was not part of Wellington's make-up – but a continuation of his normal behaviour, calculated to reassure his allies; in addition to this everyone of military significance was at the ball, which made a ready-gathered staff conference. There was much movement to and fro during the evening – despatches arriving, orders given, officers leaving to prepare their troops.

When news arrived that Napoleon was advancing rapidly up the road from Charleroi and had practically reached Quatre Bras, Wellington ordered his armies to concentrate there, left the ball at 3.00 am for two hours sleep, and set out for Quatre Bras, twenty miles due south of Brussels, at dawn on 16th June. He found the Prussians drawn up at Ligny, a few miles east of Quatre Bras, facing Napoleon's army of about equal numbers. At Quatre Bras itself, Marshal Ney had advanced on the Belgians under the Prince of Orange, and was within an ace of sweeping through the defences and on to Brussels. At almost the last moment the British troops under General Picton arrived in sufficient numbers to meet the first onslaught, and from then on the Allied strength increased as the French attacks were maintained. Ney, starved of reinforcements by Napoleon's insistence on keeping 20,000 men to add to his own attack on the Prussians at Ligny, could not break through. His cavalry broke on the British infantry squares time and again, but at last Wellington's forces had built up enough for him to order an advance. Contesting every inch, the French retired. By nightfall the battle was over, neither side having gained any clear advantage, and both having lost nearly 5,000 troops.

WATERLOO 18th JUNE 1815

Meanwhile at Ligny the Prussians under Blücher had been very badly mauled by Napoleon, as Wellington had foreseen, and it was touch and go whether the whole Prussian force would decide to stay or make for home. Only the indomitable courage of the aged Blücher kept them together and in contact with Wellington as they fell back northwards about eighteen miles to Wavre. Wellington, when he received this disquieting news, knew that he too must fall back. Already in his mind was the position where he would finally stand against

Waterloo

'Copenhagen', Wellington's favourite horse, which he rode at Waterloo, is buried at Stratfield Saye.

Napoleon — that same position he had looked at in his first reconnaissances months ago: the village of Waterloo. In the morning of the 17th he retreated; at the same time, Napoleon's Marshal Grouchy with 30,000 men was tracking Blücher's retreat. Napoleon himself advanced to join Ney in another and final attack on Quatre Bras, only to find the bird had flown except for an effective rearguard commanded by Lord Uxbridge. At this moment the weather broke into a violent storm, and the countryside rapidly became a quagmire.

Wellington went on to his chosen position at Waterloo, his main forces out of sight behind a ridge in his well-proven way. By midnight he was in bed in his cottage headquarters. His troops were camped, in mud and pouring rain, behind the east-west road leading to Wavre. In front of their position on the right was the fortified chateau of Hougomont in which a strong detachment of the Guards was stationed; a little closer and directly in front, on the main road from which Napoleon was to come, was the farmhouse of La Haye Sainte, garrisoned by German riflemen.

Wellington

A print of the chateau of Hougomont, where Wellington stationed a detachment of Guards, who only narrowly prevented its capture after bombardment by the French.

At six the next morning, 18th June 1815, Wellington rode round his 67,000 troops. They had spent a miserable wet night but were much cheered by his presence and the rain had now stopped. Meanwhile, Napoleon had decided, fatally, not to recall the 30,000 troops with which Grouchy had been shadowing Marshal Blücher, and he reviewed his 72,000 men in the fitful sunshine.

At 11.25 am the battle of Waterloo began with a French bombardment of the British infantry on the slopes facing them. A strong force immediately followed up with an attack on the chateau of Hougomont, only to be beaten back by the furious fire of the Guards inside. Renewing the attack, the French burst through the main gate; in the desperate hand-to-hand fighting, four officers and a sergeant succeeded in closing the gate again – which act, implied Wellington afterwards, was instrumental in winning the whole battle. For an hour and a half Prince Jerome, Napoleon's younger brother, threw waves of troops at the chateau with appalling losses; under Wellington's personal supervision it held firm.

Wellington rode off at 1.00 pm to his command post in the

middle of the line. Half an hour later Ney's infantry, 16,000 strong, advanced like a juggernaut up the muddy slopes towards the centre, preceded by another violent bombardment. They slaughtered and scattered the Dutch and Belgians who were first in line and rolled on to meet Picton's Highlanders who rose up from behind the slope. Outnumbered as the Scots were, the situation was critical. At this moment Wellington ordered the cavalry to charge and the whole of the Heavy Brigade and the Union Brigade (English, Scottish and Irish cavalry) swept past the reeling Highlanders and fell on the French infantry in the greatest charge ever made. Among them were the Scots Greys who, maddened with excitement, charged on and on until they were cut off and almost totally destroyed. But the task had been done: the French had been hurled back from the ridge they were so close to taking.

It was 3.00 pm and Blücher's forward troops had been seen approaching from the east. Ney ordered a massive bombardment on the centre of Wellington's troops as a preliminary to an assault on La Haye Sainte, a key position for both sides. The artillery fire caused considerable casualties and Wellington withdrew part of his line to fill the gaps. Ney, mistaking the movement for a retreat, fatally launched his whole force of light cavalry, unsupported, at the British infantry. Calmly the British squares formed. The gunners in front fired until the last moment and ran back into the squares. The infantry waited until the French cavalry were thirty yards away and then sent volley after volley into the densely packed masses. Not a square broke, and Ney called off the shattered remains of his light cavalry. To the astonishment of the British he then launched his heavy cavalry in exactly the same way – with the same result. By this time casualties were enormous, on the Allied side as well as the French. Wellington moved about the battlefield, rallying troops, retiring into a square when he was threatened by a French charge, moving forces here and there. At about 5.00 pm new attacks of mixed cavalry and infantry were launched; again the squares stood firm and the guns wreaked havoc among the attackers.

But now Napoleon decided on an all-out attack on La Haye Sainte by the road. In spite of an incredibly heroic defence by the 376 members of the King's German Legion, it fell to overwhelming waves launched by Ney. On went the French

Wellington

The meeting of Wellington and Blücher after the battle of Waterloo, on the road at La Belle Alliance.

troops up the ridge to engage in the bloodiest hand-to-hand fighting of the day. The British infantry was severely weakened by now and the sudden chance was present that a determined French attack here would mean an overall victory for Napoleon. Unaccountably Napoleon hesitated for half an hour, allowing Wellington to bring up to the shattered centre the few reinforcements he had left, and by the strength of his own personality to instil a new confidence into his army.

At last Napoleon launched the Old Guard, his veterans who had never failed in an attack. Although decimated by accurate gunfire, they closed ranks and advanced in massive walls up the ridge to the rhythm of their drums. At Wellington's signal, 1,500 of the 1st Foot Guards who had been lying concealed just behind the ridge rose up and poured volley after volley into Napoleon's veterans at point blank range. They wavered and began to move back, attacked on the flank by the Light Brigade as well as by the Guards in front. It was the first time that Napoleon's veteran 'moustaches' had retreated in battle and it had a shattering effect on the morale of his army. Nonetheless,

Waterloo

at this point the battle still hung in the balance. Then suddenly, at about 7.30 in the evening, the Prussians arrived and fell on Napoleon's extreme right flank. Seizing his chance, Wellington waved his hat in the air and his whole army rose up and streamed down the hill.

There was still frightful slaughter to come, but the day was won. Napoleon, after a vain attempt to rally the remnants of his army, fled. Wellington and Blücher met on the road at La Belle Alliance at 9.00 pm. Waterloo was over, but at dreadful cost: Wellington lost 15,000; Blücher 7,000; Napoleon 25,000. The memory of the battlefield as it was that night never left the Iron Duke, who wept at the long list of his dead friends and comrades. Later he sat down to write the Waterloo Despatch (the original is still owned by the family), describing to Lord Bathurst, the War Minister, the four days which had just ended. Dispassionate and factual, it created unhappy controversy at home by its shortage of the traditional praise of individual commanders and regiments. Later he said two significant things. On the morning following the battle, in a rare outburst of truth

Wellington

about his own part, he said: 'By God! I don't think it would have done if I had not been there!' Then, in a letter, he wrote: 'I hope to God I have fought my last battle'. He had — at least in the military sense.

OCCUPATION 1815

A further title — Prince of Waterloo — was added by King William of the Netherlands to the long list of Wellington's ennoblements. Napoleon meanwhile rushed back to Paris to bolster his cracking image, but in vain; for the last time he left Paris, and for the second time Louis XVIII returned to the throne of France. Napoleon was exiled to St Helena where he died in 1821. Wellington, his conqueror, was voted about £200,000 by Parliament and promised a fine house in England. He was by now installed in Paris (where Kitty joined him in October) to represent England with Lord Castlereagh at the Peace Conference which opened in July. The conference was in fact more stormy than peaceful, but it appointed Wellington to command the army of occupation, which he did from a headquarters at Cambrai and a town house on the Champs Elysées.

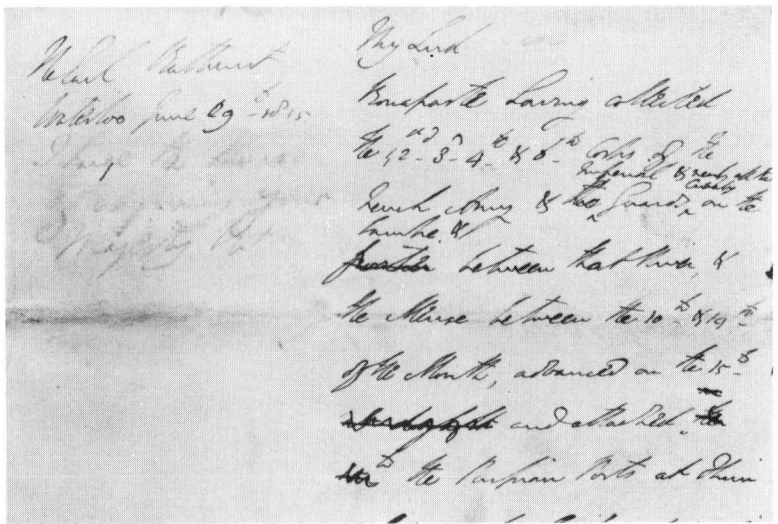

The beginning of the despatch sent by Wellington after Waterloo to the War Minister, Lord Bathurst.

Parliamentary career

STRATFIELD SAYE AND APSLEY HOUSE

While Wellington virtually ruled France, things in England were far from well. The war had made her rich, but the tide was not long in turning once it was over; by the spring of 1816 there was poverty and unrest almost everywhere. William Cobbett, a leading radical figure, started a popular agitation against taxation without representation. Reform was the byword of the day – reform of the unjust and creaking system of suffrage – and it led to bitter scenes of marches and rioting, confrontations of working men and troops, hangings and deportations. Wellington, at that stage and at that distance, found most of his sympathies with the masses rather than the masters. He was a soldier first and last, and his necessary contacts with politics at high level had not enamoured him of the system.

1817 was a better year than 1816. Waterloo Day was celebrated in great style and included the opening of Waterloo Bridge. More important to Wellington, his search for a country house was at last successful. On the recommendation of his architect Benjamin Wyatt he accepted the offer of Lord Rivers to sell his estate at Stratfield Saye in north Hampshire, and for £263,000 the nation bought it for him, setting up a Parliamentary Trust (which survived unchanged until 1971). Wellington's intention was to build a much grander house in the park, and designs were produced in some detail. However, the cost – another quarter of a million or so – and Kitty's immediate and continuing affection for Stratfield Saye House prevented this scheme from being realised.

By the following year, unrest in Paris (including one determined attempt on his life) and his own long-held conviction that the occupation of France should be ended, coupled with a clear improvement in France's financial affairs,

Above: Stratfield Saye House, Hampshire, was bought by the nation for the Duke in 1817. This drawing shows it as altered by Wellington.

Left: Apsley House, London, at the time of its purchase by Wellington from his brother, 1817.

led to the congress of Aix-la-Chapelle in October and agreement on terms. Wellington returned to London where he bought, from his somewhat impoverished elder brother, Apsley House at Hyde Park Corner. Into this mansion poured treasures from all over Europe — an enormous naked statue of Napoleon from the Louvre, a silver dinner service from the people of Portugal, a huge service of porcelain from the King of Prussia, another from Louis of France; and countless other gifts. Many of these can be seen there today since the 7th Duke of Wellington gave the house and its contents to the nation. It was opened to the public in 1952.

MASTER-GENERAL OF THE ORDINANCE

At this moment, to most of his friends' surprise (and in many cases sadness) Wellington entered serious politics, accepting the position of Master-General of the Ordinance. It seemed to be a complete reversal of all his principles: how could he equate his distrust of politics and politicians with this action? In fact, he made it clear that he would have nothing to do with party politics, and that his action in taking a ministerial position in Lord Liverpool's cabinet was prompted by a certainty that there was nobody who could do this particular job better than he could. Such was the universal awe and respect for him that his motives were accepted without question.

One characteristic explains the whole of Wellington's parliamentary career, which otherwise appears to be a succession of policy reversals on major issues; reversals which almost invariably brought him into direct conflict with the people, or the Tory party to which his upbringing and position pointed him. That characteristic was an unshakable determination to do what was right for the country. That determination led him to bolster up an ailing monarchy; to set his face sternly and repressively against Parliamentary reform, and then to champion it when he felt that the country needed this radical change; to put down violence and revolt with fierce ruthlessness. Indeed, one of his acts after taking office in 1819 has come to be known as the Massacre of Peterloo. This was a year when the evils of the system — Corn Laws that kept foreign corn out in spite of disastrous harvests in England, savage sentences for minor offences, poverty widespread and political agitation everywhere — were particularly in evidence. In August

Wellington

a huge meeting was organised in Manchester to discuss political reform. 80,000 people gathered, an assembly large enough to persuade the local magistrate to call in the military. Through misunderstanding or over-enthusiasm, the cavalry charged the unarmed mass, which was confined in a square and unable to get away. There were 500 casualties – men, women and children.

CAROLINE OF BRUNSWICK

The monarchy was going through a particularly bad patch at this time. In January 1820 King George III died, to be succeeded by George IV, who had for years been separated from his wife, Caroline of Brunswick. A nationwide controversy broke out as to whether she should be allowed to become Queen. George produced evidence of her infidelity and scandalous behaviour and introduced a bill to effect a divorce; Caroline announced her intention of taking her rightful place as Queen. Wellington, whose transparent uprightness made him the only possible choice as an arbiter, was appointed to achieve a settlement with Caroline's representatives. The matter dragged through Parliament in a macabre and undignified way, with Wellington taking the brunt of the mob's disapproval. Caroline was tried before Parliament, but the bill was eventually dropped. At George's coronation in July she was shut out of Westminster Abbey and in August she died. It was not a savoury episode, whatever the rights and wrongs, and it left Wellington with the firm conviction that the monarchy, for the good of the country and all that stemmed from it, must be maintained and reinforced however imperfect. He regarded the damage done to the Royal position as unacceptable and dangerous.

CANNING

In 1822 Wellington's old friend, the Foreign Secretary, Lord Castlereagh, committed suicide and was succeeded by the volatile and brilliant Canning – largely as a result of Wellington's reserved conviction that Canning, whom he disliked, was the right man for the country at the time, and his subsequent persuasion of the King. Wellington himself went off in Castlereagh's place to the Congress of Verona (another attempt to solve the problems of Europe by discussion); but not before he had suddenly become stone deaf in one ear as the result of a catastrophic piece of doctoring. It was almost the first time in his life, since his extreme youth, that he had been ill. 'I am very tired of being sick, never having been so before' he wrote. 'Even the strength of my Iron constitution tells now against me.' He must have been a difficult patient. He had a special ear-trumpet in the form of a walking stick made; it is still at Stratfield Saye.

Wellington at this period was a close confidant of the King, restraining or persuading him as seemed to him best for the country. Relations with Canning deteriorated as Canning became more and more powerful and every now and again the suggestion came, from this powerful quarter or that, that Wellington was Lord Liverpool's natural successor as prime minister.

The time for that was not yet, however. Looming on the horizon was the problem of Ireland with which the Duke, as an Irishman at least in origin, was much concerned. His brother Lord Wellesley became Lord Lieutenant in 1821. Frightful poverty, the perennial Catholic-Protestant violence and an increasing hatred of the English (particularly the absentee landlords) kept the unhappy country in a constant state of ferment. Wellington almost decided that armed pacification was the only solution, but in his usual dispassionate way he also gave serious thought to the reform of the whole system of government there. Increasingly he became convinced that while Ireland must remain a Protestant country, the suppression of the Catholics, whose champion Daniel O'Connell was the chief thorn in the government's flesh, must somehow be relieved.

COMMANDER-IN-CHIEF 1827

In January 1827 the Duke of York, commander-in-chief of the British army since before Wellington went to Spain as Sir Arthur Wellesley, died; and the following month Lord Liverpool, the Prime Minister, had a stroke. (He was, incidentally, Lord Warden of the Cinque Ports and when he died in December 1828 Wellington asked to be appointed, and derived great pleasure for the rest of his life from Walmer Castle, the official residence.) The immediate question was whether Wellington would assume one or both of these offices. The first he took almost automatically, for there was no other possible candidate. On the subject of the second, the King havered for a full month of intrigue and counter intrigue. Then,

Wellington

to Wellington's mortification, he called Canning to form a government.

Wellington promptly resigned both from the Cabinet and his position as commander-in-chief, and precipitated the resignation of many others. There was a good deal of public feeling against him, which was heightened when the first attempt to bring in a Corn Law to restrict the import of foreign corn was defeated, apparently because Wellington was against it (in fact he was trying for a better deal for the agricultural poor whom he championed). Suddenly Canning was ill, and only a hundred days after he had taken office, he died on 8th August 1827. Wellington, still declaiming that he was a soldier and not a politician, accepted his old position of commander-in-chief of the army at the King's request.

PRIME MINISTER 1828

After a few months, the stop-gap administration of Lord Goderich fell, and on 9th January 1828 King George sent for Wellington to form a government. He was, almost in spite of himself, Prime Minister. Among the members of the Cabinet which he formed were Peel as Leader of the House of Commons and Home Secretary, and Lord Palmerston as Secretary for War.

Much of his first year of office as Prime Minister was taken up with the ever-present Irish question. His private convictions that the Catholics must be emancipated had not yet been shown in public, and a head-on conflict at an election in County Clare between Wellington's candidate and Daniel O'Connell himself made the situation suddenly much more tense. O'Connell was of course a Catholic, and a Catholic was forbidden by law to sit in Parliament. He was nonetheless elected by a large majority, and proceeded in effect to become the popular ruler of Ireland. It looked as if a showdown was imminent, but solutions were delayed beyond 1828 by the King's ill health and the sheer complexity of the problem. One of the worst difficulties – getting Peel on his side – was overcome by January 1829, and the following month the Duke's policy of Catholic emancipation was at last made public.

In the succeeding few weeks Wellington stood by his principle against attacks, from the King downwards, which could have brought the career of a less determined man to a sudden end. Indeed, the situation led directly to the one and

Left: The Duke of Wellington at the coronation of George IV in 1821.

Right: Katherine (Kitty) Pakenham, Duchess of Wellington, drawn in 1814.

Left: The library at Stratfield Saye House drawn by Kitty, Duchess of Wellington.

Wellington

A cartoon of Wellington's duel at Battersea with Lord Winchilsea, who had attacked his policy of Catholic emancipation.

only duel which the Duke fought during his lifetime. In March Lord Winchilsea, one of the leaders of the anti-Catholic faction, made such violent and damaging accusations against him that Wellington was eventually compelled to issue a challenge. The duel, at Battersea, ended in each party firing deliberately wide, and honour was satisfied.

Catholic emancipation was a battle won, but another campaign was imminent. Poverty in both the countryside and the rapidly increasing towns was becoming desperate, partly through a series of bad harvests and cruel winters. For the moment there was no solution that would not antagonise his main supporters in the Tory party: and although he privately helped his tenants at Stratfield Saye, he rather short-sightedly remained convinced that the country as a whole was in good shape, and getting better. On 26th June 1830 King George IV died, and was succeeded by his brother as William IV. William, friendly and anxious to please, had scarcely sat on the throne

Opposite: The Duke with Harriet Arbuthnot, 1834. Mrs Arbuthnot was for many years a close confidante of Wellington, but there was no trace of scandal about their relationship.

Wellington

before there was a sudden burst of revolution throughout Europe. An uprising in Paris threw out King Charles and replaced him with Louis Philippe, the 'Citizen King'. The whole of Britain caught the reform fever afresh. The extreme poverty of the labouring classes in England led to riots, cases of rick burning and machine-breaking during the autumn of 1830. But in a dramatic speech to the House of Lords at the beginning of November the Duke firmly declared himself against a Reform Bill. 'I am not only not prepared to bring forward any measure of this nature, but I will at once declare that . . . I shall always feel it my duty to resist such measures when proposed by others.' One could scarcely have made it clearer than that.

The effects of this unexpected setting of Wellington's face against reforms which practically everyone else felt must merely be a matter of time were immediate and widespread. Mobs in London hissed him whenever he appeared; sackfuls of threatening letters arrived; a state visit by the King to the City of London had to be cancelled because of a real risk of assassination. Apsley House itself was barricaded. The Duke took to carrying an umbrella ending in a sharp spike to protect himself from attack.

On 15th November Wellington's government was defeated in a minor debate which was made the occasion for a showdown. Wellington resigned the next day and was never Prime Minister again. Lord Grey formed a government with a new mix of Radicals and Tories, ready for the reforms which had to come.

The final years

THE REFORM BILL

Wellington was now more free to pursue the interests of two of his other positions; Constable of the Tower of London (from 1826) and Lord Warden of the Cinque Ports (from 1829). To both he brought his characteristic energy and attention to detail. Walmer Castle (which he loved) saw a lot of him, and he found plenty to occupy him there, for the sphere of responsibility of the Lord Warden was then extensive – pilotage, discipline, harbour works and salvage among them. But among this semi-official activity he needed to give attention to his own county of Hampshire, where rioting and arson was increasing under the direction of the mysterious 'Captain Swing'.

Even the Duke's pew at Stratfield Saye church was set on fire. As Lord Lieutenant and the chief anti-reformer, Wellington set about the task with an iron hand, organising posses of neighbouring landowners which resulted in hangings, floggings and deportations for the rioters they caught.

Meanwhile Grey's government worked on a Reform Bill which was introduced by Lord John Russell in March 1831. Sweeping reform of the pocket borough system (which in effect allowed certain large landowners to control several constituencies) were proposed, and in redistributing seats the voteless large towns such as Liverpool were to have representation for the first time. Wellington, as he had said he would, spoke against it. The second reading produced a government majority of one; Lord Grey, not wishing to risk a defeat at the next stage, decided to ask the King to dissolve Parliament, which was effected in an absolute bedlam of noise on 22nd April.

At this traumatic moment Kitty, Duchess of Wellington, died at Apsley House after a long illness; she is buried in the family vault at Stratfield Saye church. On the 27th, while she was lying dead at Apsley House, a Reform Bill mob threw stones through most of the windows.

The new election resulted in a clear-cut victory for the reformers, but nonetheless the opposition to it (still led by Wellington) won the day and the Second Reform Bill was defeated by the Lords on 8th October. The Duke's effigy was burned at Tyburn, and again the mob threw stones through the windows of Apsley House. Another attempt at a Reform Act the following April was once more defeated by the Lords. Wellington was asked by the King to form a government, but he could not find the support he needed. Now at last he saw that his resolute and unyielding stand against reform was leading nowhere and with singular courage he gave way when Britain actually appeared to be on the brink of a revolution. Abstaining at the next vote in the House of Lords, and followed by a large body of Tories, he allowed the Reform Bill through in June 1832.

There followed two years of uneasy bickering between Commons and Lords, with the Irish question appearing on one of its regular forays. An event which gave him great pleasure during this time was his election, amid scenes of real public acclaim, as Chancellor of Oxford University in 1834. More than once Wellington was asked to become Prime Minister, as Parliamentary crisis after crisis brought loose coalitions to an end; each time he refused, being unable to see the support he needed to govern effectively.

In 1834 he lost his dearest friend, Harriet Arbuthnot, with whom he had exchanged views and news for most of his adult life, and who was certainly closer to him than any other human being. Her death was a grievous blow to him, far more so than his wife's death three years earlier. It is very unlikely, as has been suggested, that Wellington had any sort of illicit relationships with Mrs Arbuthnot. He was not averse to a pretty face, but this was a meeting of minds – hers shrewd and lively, his accurate, penetrating and denied of the intellectual stimulus which Kitty had been unable to provide. The correspondence between them (the originals of which are still kept by the family) is the best source of his real thoughts and feelings which he disguised from the rest of the world. Wellington had the reputation of answering every letter he received by return, and, from the

Apsley House as altered by the Duke. The shadow on the facade is of an enormous equestrian statue of him, later removed to Aldershot.

enormous number of letters which have survived, this is probably very largely true.

In the autumn of 1834, Wellington (having refused the Premiership) took office as Foreign Secretary in Peel's government. It was an even more uneasy administration than most recent ones had been, and in April 1835 Peel resigned – and with him of course, Wellington; it was the last time he was to hold office. At sixty-eight he was active and in excellent health, except for occasional 'seizures' after hard exercise (usually riding) and increasing deafness. His popularity too was high (it moved, not unexpectedly as will have been seen, in inverse proportion to his political activity).

On 20th June 1837, two days after the now traditional Waterloo banquet which was held every year at Apsley House, the King died, to be succeeded by his eighteen-year-old niece Princess Victoria. At her coronation, the cheers for the Duke were louder than the cheers for the new young Queen: she had some revenge a little later when she absolutely refused to lose all her court ladies (as was constitutionally *de rigeur* on a

Wellington

An equestrian statue in silver of the Duke of Wellington by Robert Garrard.

change of government) in spite of both Wellington's and Peel's urgings. Disenchantment with the old Duke continued to the date of her wedding with Prince Albert in 1840, when some pressure had to be applied by her favourite Lord Melbourne to persuade her to invite him at all. By the time of his death however, the Duke was admired and respected by the Queen and had become a close and dear friend.

THE CORN LAWS AND IRELAND

In the previous October Wellington suffered a stroke and in February another. It looked as if the end of the Duke as a public figure (at the least) was imminent, and he himself began to talk of retirement. But it was a temporary setback only.

In 1841 a new Conservative government under Peel was formed and for the first time for years it was a strong government with a substantial majority. Wellington, with a choice of office open to him, decided to remain Leader of the House of Lords but without any other appointment. It was a situation which did not last long, though the change was unexpected; in August 1842 Lord Hill, Commander-in-Chief of the Army, resigned and Wellington once more took over control of the British Army, at the age of seventy-three, while still retaining his position without portfolio in the Cabinet.

His two lives, at this time parliamentary and landowning, often overlapped. There was deep unrest in the country through bad harvests, while the Corn Laws, though somewhat relaxed, still forced the price of food up to an unjust level. Riots broke out frequently in the worst affected areas, and mass arrests followed. Politically, improvements were gradually made in the frightful conditions of the industrial and agricultural workers – a Factory Bill, a Mines Bill. Ireland as always was in a state of seething unrest fomented by Daniel O'Connell to undo the union, and Wellington prepared for out-and-out war to defend it. Distress on a scale never before seen even in Ireland struck first; in the autumn of 1845 the potato crop failed. Potatoes were the staple diet of the Irish poor, and a complete failure meant automatic starvation. Peel saw that the only permanent solution was to repeal the Corn Laws entirely. Wellington, asked for his opinion, gave it – against repeal; but he would support Peel if he decided to legislate. After resignation and recall, Peel finally got his Act repealing the Corn

Laws passed in May 1846; the most important and telling speech in support was made by Wellington.

DEATH AND TRIBUTES

The last six years of his life were comparatively uneventful: advising and supporting the Queen and her Consort; attending to his duties as commander-in-chief; writing letters. Wellington spent the last weeks of his life, in 1852, at his favourite Walmer Castle. There was business to be done as Lord Warden, friends to see, more letters as always to write. On 13th September after a full day, with visits from his grandchildren, he went to bed. He woke up feeling unwell, and gradually sank through the morning. He died, sitting in his favourite armchair, at 3.25 on 14th September 1852. His body was embalmed while preparations were made for the greatest state funeral that England has ever experienced. He lay for two days at Walmer for the local people to pay their respects, and was then carried to London to lie in state in Chelsea Hospital. The funeral procession, with the huge and ornate car (weighing 18 tons) which carried the coffin, was a spectacle watched by more than a million people. The route led to St Paul's Cathedral, and there the hero of Waterloo was laid to rest.

For nearly forty years, between the series of brilliant victories against Napoleon's troops in the Spanish Peninsula and his death at Walmer Castle, Arthur Wellesley was the most famous living Englishman. From the time of his final defeat of Napoleon at Waterloo, his stature was unrivalled throughout Europe. In a long life (he was eighty-three when he died) he spent more than half of it where he was not only at the top of the tree, but was in effect the tree itself: 'He was the GREATEST man this country ever produced...' lamented Queen Victoria on his death, and few of her subjects — except perhaps the most radical of his political opponents — would have disagreed with her. Historians, while acknowledging his military genius, have not been over-kind to him as a statesman, and his rather spiky personality has not endeared him to generations that had no opportunity to bask in his glories. Nonetheless his position as one of the most important characters in the story of Britain has never been doubted, which makes all the more remarkable the fact that he was perhaps the least personally ambitious public figure that Britain has ever produced.

Above: Wellington with his grandchildren in the library at Stratfield Saye House, 1852.

Below: Walmer Castle, Kent, the Duke's official residence as Lord Warden of the Cinque Ports. Here he died in 1852.

Wellington

His political life, which lasted for more than thirty-five years, seems to have been characterised by actions which made the common people hate him. During his campaigns, as supreme commander he could afford to make up his own mind and then to act without consultation, and the results of his secretive decisions were quickly evidenced in victory after victory. In politics, with a party and a country to carry, the effect was a good deal less happy.

The sheer volume of material which stems from his life and doings is prodigious. He was painted scores of times (unwillingly as a rule: he could not understand why everyone wanted a picture of him); and sketches, cartoons, allegories, prints, busts, statues and popular souvenirs were produced in numbers beyond counting. Much of this material has survived and there are comprehensive collections at Stratfield Saye House; at the Wellington Museum at Apsley House, his London home; and at Walmer Castle.

An amazing quantity of written material documents his life, but he had a devastating way with those whom he considered were interfering in his private affairs. 'The Duke of Wellington has nothing to say', he wrote at the age of seventy-one to Sir J. E. Alexander 'to the forty or fifty Lives of Himself which are at present in the course of being written.' Among the most recent published works on his life is the excellent two-volume biography by Elizabeth Longford.

His concern about military details resulted in the Wellington boot (a name later extended from the original leather calf-length boot to the present familiar rubber one). Towns and cities throughout the world bear his name. The species of tree called Wellingtonia (a type of sequoia) was named after him, as were a blackcurrant, a tulip, an apple and a rose – and doubtless other horticultural products as well. Wellington College (since founded in his honour, and Wellington Barracks (since demolished) carried his name. The number of public houses and streets which bear his name is almost beyond counting. It seems safe to say that the great Duke of Wellington will not be forgotten. If ever a man deserved his niche in the halls of fame, it is he.

Opposite: the Duke of Wellington in old age.

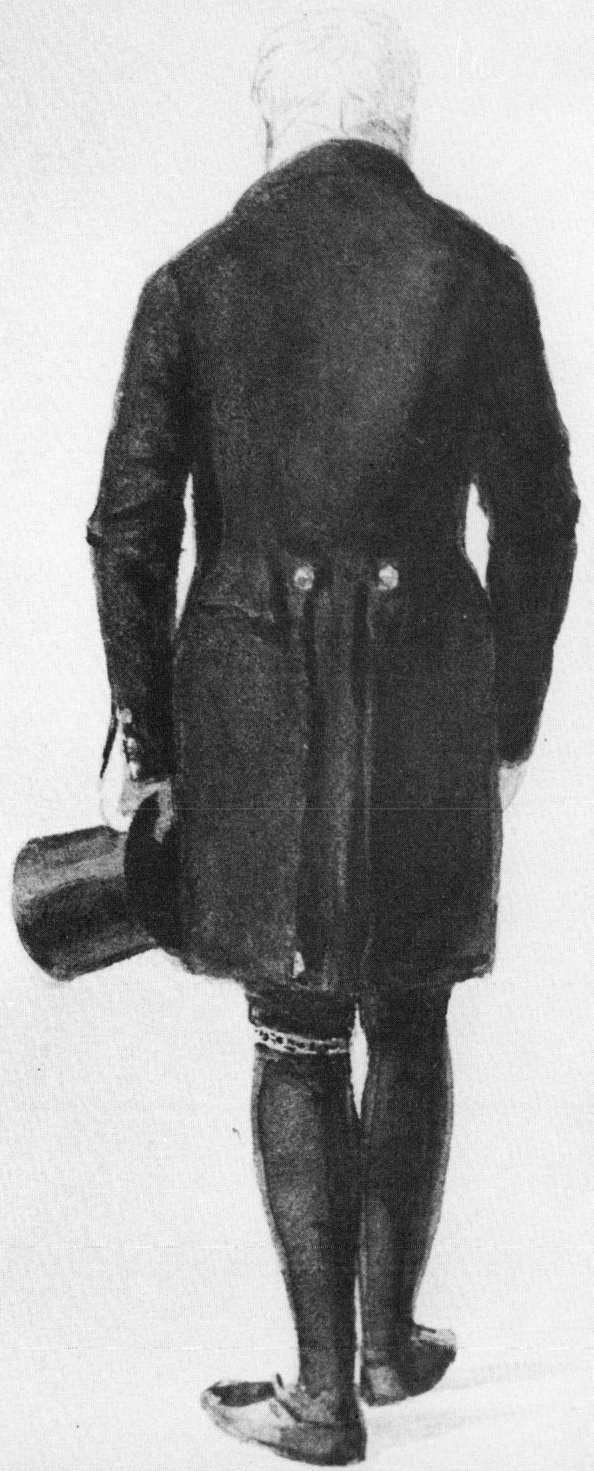

Wellington

THE PRINCIPAL EVENTS OF WELLINGTON'S LIFE

1769	Hon. Arthur Wesley born. *Napoleon Bonaparte born*
1787	Gazetted as Ensign
1790	MP for Trim, Ireland
1793	*France declares war on Britain*
1796	Promoted Colonel. Sails for India
1798	Family name changed to Wellesley
1803	Battle of Assaye
1804	Knighted (Order of the Bath)
1805	Returns to England. *Battle of Trafalgar*
1806	Marries Katherine Pakenham
1807	Chief Secretary for Ireland
1808	Portugal: battle of Vimeiro
1809	Battle of Talavera. Created Viscount
1812	Storming of Ciudad Rodrigo. Created Earl. Battle of Salamanca. Created Marquess
1813	Battle of Vitoria. Created Knight of the Garter and Field Marshal
1814	*Abdication of Napoleon.* Created Duke
1815	*Napoleon escapes from Elba.* Battle of Quatre Bras. Battle of Waterloo
1818	Master General of the Ordinance
1819	*Peterloo Massacre*
1821	*Death of Napoleon*
1827	Commander-in-Chief
1828	Prime Minister
1829	Lord Warden of the Cinque Ports. Duel with Lord Winchilsea. Resignation
1831	Death of Duchess of Wellington
1832	*Reform Act passed*
1834	Foreign Secretary
1837	*Death of William IV and accession of Victoria*
1842	Commander-in-Chief again
1846	*Repeal of the Corn Laws*
1852	Death of Wellington at Walmer Castle. Buried at St Paul's

Opposite: The Duke of Wellington's funeral procession passing Apsley House.

BIBLIOGRAPHY

Wellington: The Years of the Sword; Elizabeth Longford; Weidenfeld & Nicolson, 1969.

Wellington: Pillar of State; Elizabeth Longford; Weidenfeld & Nicolson, 1972.

There have been many biographies of the great Duke of Wellington. The standard work today is without question the recently published two-volume work mentioned above.

The Duke of Wellington, A Pictorial Survey of his Life; Victor Percival; Victoria and Albert Museum, 1969. (Profusely illustrated with a great variety of material.)

Wellington and His Friends: Letters of the 1st Duke selected and edited by the 7th Duke of Wellington; Victor Percival; 1965.

The Wellington Despatch; Reginald Colby; Victoria and Albert Museum, 1965.

Wellington; Reginald Colby; English Life Publications Ltd. (A summary of the 1st Duke's career and an account of Apsley House. Largely pictorial.)

INDEX
Page numbers in italic refer to illustrations

Albuera 14
Almeida 14
Angers 5
Apsley House 17, *28,* 29, 36, 37, 38, *39,* 44
Arbuthnot, Harriet *35,* 38
Assaye 6-7
Badajoz 14
Bayonne 18
Beresford 14
Blücher 19, 20, 21, 22, 23, *24,* 25
Bonaparte, Joseph 8, 12, *15,* 16, 17
Bonaparte, Napoleon 5, 8, 10, 13, 15, 17, 18, 19-26
Brussels 5, 19, 20
Burgos 15, 16
Burrard, Sir Henry 9
Bussaco 12
Canning 30, 31, 32
Caroline of Brunswick 30
Castlereagh, Lord 26, 30
Catholic emancipation 31, 32, 34
Charleroi 19, 20
Cintra, Convention of 10, 11
Ciudad Rodrigo *13,* 14, 15
Commander-in-Chief 31, 32, 41, 42
Copenhagen 8
Copenhagen (horse) 8, *21*
Corn Laws 29, 32, 41-42
Cuesta, General 11
Douro, Passage of 11
Eton 5
Ferdinand VII 8, 17
Fuentes de Onoro 14
Funeral of Wellington 42, *47*
George IV 30, 31, 32, 34
Goderich, Lord 32
Grey, Lord 36, 37
Grouchy 21, 22
Hougomont 21, 22
India 6-7
Ireland 6, 7, 8, 10, 11, 31, 32, 41
La Haye Sainte 21, 23
Ligny 20
Lisbon 9, 12
Liverpool, Lord 29, 31
Lord Warden of Cinque Ports 31, 37, 42
Louis XVIII 19, 26, 29

Madrid 11, 14
Marmont 14
Massena 12, 13, 14
Master-General of Ordinance 29
Mornington, Earl of 5
Ney 12, 20, 21, 23
Nivelle, River 18
O'Connell, Daniel 31, 32, 41
Oporto 11
Palmerston 32
Pamplona 17
Paris 18, 19, 26, 27, 36
Peel 32, 39, 41
Peninsular War 9-18
Peterloo 29-30
Picton 20, 23
Prime Minister 32-36
Pyrenees 16, 17, 18
Quatre Bras 19-20, 21
Reform 27, 29, 36, 37, 38
Rolica 9
Russell, Lord John 37
St Helena 7, 26
Salamanca 14, 15, 16
San Sebastian 17
Seringapatam 6
Soult 11, 14, 17, 18
Stratfield Saye 8, 17, 27, *28,* 31, 34, 37, 38, *43,* 44
Talavera 11-12
Tippoo Sultan 6
Torres Vedras 9, *10,* 12-13
Toulouse 18
Uxbridge, Lord 21
Valladolid 16
Verona, Congress of 30
Victor, Marshal 11
Victoria, Queen 39, 41, 42
Vienna, Congress of 18, 19
Vimeiro 9-10
Vitoria 16-17
Walmer Castle 31, 37, 42, *43,* 44
Waterloo 18, 20-26
Wavre 20-21
Wellesley, Marquess of 6, 31
Wellington, Duchess of (Kitty Pakenham) 7, 18, 26, *33,* 37, 38
William IV 34, 37, 38, 39
Winchilsea, Lord 34